BIG BOOK OF
PESTO

BIG BOOK OF
PESTO

EBURY
PRESS

1 3 5 7 9 10 8 6 4 2

Published in 2013 by Ebury Press, an imprint of Ebury Publishing

A Random House Group Company

The Random House Group Limited Reg. No. 954009

Addresses for companies within the Random House Group can be found
at www.randomhouse.co.uk

A CIP catalogue record for this book is available from the British Library

The Random House Group Limited supports the Forest Stewardship
Council® (FSC®), the leading international forest-certification
organisation. Our books carrying the FSC label are printed on
FSC®-certified paper. FSC is the only forest-certification scheme
supported by the leading environmental organisations, including
Greenpeace. Our paper procurement policy can be found at
www.randomhouse.co.uk/environment

To buy books by your favourite authors and register for offers visit
www.randomhouse.co.uk

For more recipe inspiration visit www.sacla.co.uk

Recipe development by Louisa Carter
Project editor: Roxanne Mackey
Production: Lucy Harrison
Design by ClarkevanMeurs Design Ltd
Photography by Clive Bozzard-Hill
Food styling by Mitzie Wilson
Props styling by Clare Macdonald

Printed and bound in China by C&C Offset Printing Co., Ltd

ISBN 9780091951825

Carlo and Lorenzo as young boys

Our shared passion for authentic, irresistible Italian food is still what drives us to experiment with new technologies and new product ideas. For example, solar panels mean our fresh pesto is made using the warmth of the Italian sunshine! We use only the finest, freshest ingredients, we recreate mainly traditional Italian recipes, and we ensure that all our products are made in Italy.

We hope the *Sacla' Big Book of Pesto* will inspire your own creativity, flexibility and enthusiasm in the kitchen – *buon appetito!*

to his products being found in homes and kitchens in over 50 countries across the world.

From the very beginning, each generation of the Sacla' family has built on the company's spirit of creativity, flexibility and enthusiasm – everything that's at the heart of our philosophy and culture today.

COOK'S NOTES

Unless otherwise specified:

All eggs are medium and should preferably be free range or organic

All onions and garlic should be peeled

Milk should be semi-skimmed

Our President Cavaliere del Lavoro Lorenzo Ercole has literally grown up with the business – both he and Sacla' were born in 1939.

CONTENTS

Secondo and Piera Ercole, our founders, with their two sons, Carlo (left) and Lorenzo (right)

AT SACLA' we get out of bed in the morning for Pesto. It's our all-consuming passion and our reason for being. So, perhaps unsurprisingly, we're also mad about real, irresistible Italian food – especially when it's made using only the finest and freshest ingredients.

We're known as the Pesto Pioneers because about 20 years ago we brought the lovely fragrant sauce to the UK for the first time – bringing home the spirit of Italy, you could say.

As time has passed, we've indulged our palate and now have a delightful array of authentic Italian foods, from our traditional Basil Pesto to unique and innovative varieties, including Fiery Chilli and Wild Garlic Pesto.

In this book you'll find a recipe to suit everyone in your family: from a traditional pasta bake to a dinner-party showstopper. It just goes to show that with a little imagination, Pesto is not only incredibly versatile, it's an indispensable friend at home and simply downright delicious.

It all began for us in 1939 in Asti, in the fertile region of Piemonte, north-west Italy. Signor Secondo Ercole took a long look at the bounty of food grown in the Astigiano – the area surrounding Asti – and decided to share it with the world. From humble beginnings canning vegetables in Piemonte, Secondo and his wife Piera created a company that grew to become one of Italy's most progressive food companies today. He never imagined his vision would lead

1

SNACKS & NIBBLES

PESTO MAYONNAISE

A quick way to liven up mayonnaise; this is perfect for adding extra oomph to sandwiches, to serve alongside white fish or roast chicken – or even just for dunking potato wedges or chips! Experiment with different Pesto flavours and try stirring through chopped fresh herbs such as chives, basil or parsley.

For every 100 g mayonnaise swirl through 2 heaped tablespoons of Sacla' Classic Basil Pesto.

PESTO HUMMUS SERVES 4

1 garlic clove
1 x 400 g can chickpeas
5–6 tbsp extra virgin olive oil
100 g Sacla' Classic Basil Pesto
grated zest and juice of
    1 lemon
salt
Pesto Pitta Chips (see page 18)
    and crudités, such as
    carrots, cucumber, celery,
    fennel, radishes and
    peppers, to serve

For even more flavour, try adding 100 g Sacla' Char-Grilled Peppers Antipasto and some of the oil in place of the olive oil. Mix through a large handful of fresh basil leaves for extra colour and freshness.

Put the garlic into a food processor and blitz to a paste. Drain the chickpeas, reserving the water, then add to the garlic with all the other ingredients. Blitz to a rough texture. If it's a bit thick, loosen with a little of the chickpea water. Taste and adjust the seasoning with a little bit more oil, lemon, Pesto or salt, as needed.

PESTO AND PARMESAN STRAWS

MAKES AT LEAST 20

1 x 320 g packet ready-rolled
   puff pastry
flour, for dusting
4 tbsp Sacla' Pesto (Classic
   Basil, Sun-Dried Tomato,
   Roasted Pepper or Fiery
   Chilli)
75 g fresh Parmesan, grated
1 egg, lightly beaten

Preheat the oven to 220°C/425°F/gas 7.

Place the pastry on a lightly floured board. Spread half the Pesto in an even layer all over the pastry. Scatter over half the cheese. Fold the pastry in half, short sides together, and press it together firmly with your hands. Roll it out to more or less the original size.

Spread the pastry with the remaining Pesto and cover with most of the remaining Parmesan (save a bit for sprinkling on top). Fold it in half and roll it out again to its original size. Don't worry too much about getting it exactly the same size; the main thing is to make sure it's not too thick, and that the Parmesan is pressed into the pastry.

Using a sharp knife, cut the pastry into 1cm-wide strips. Take each strip and twist it from each end to make a spiral. Place the straws on a baking sheet lined with baking parchment, leaving plenty of room between each straw, as they'll puff up in size during baking. Brush first with the beaten egg and then sprinkle with the rest of the Parmesan. Bake for 10 to 12 minutes, until crisp and golden. Cool on a wire rack, or serve straight away.

SWEET POTATO WEDGES *WITH* CHILLI PESTO SOURED CREAM DIP

SERVES 3–4 AS A SNACK OR SIDE DISH

4 large sweet potatoes, cut into wedges
3 tbsp olive oil
85 g soured cream
2 heaped tbsp Sacla' Fiery Chilli Pesto
75 g Sacla' Char-Grilled Peppers Antipasto, finely chopped
flaked sea salt

Sweet potatoes vary when you cook them, so you'll find that sometimes the wedges will be crispy and sometimes a bit softer. Either way, they're completely delicious dunked in this Chilli Pesto Soured Cream Dip.

Preheat the oven to 200°C/400°F/gas 6. Toss the sweet potatoes with the oil and a good pinch of salt. Arrange them in a single layer in a roasting tray. Bake for 30 minutes, turning halfway, until they are golden at the edges and cooked through.

Meanwhile, mix together the soured cream, Pesto and peppers and spoon into a bowl. Serve the wedges while they are still hot and dunk them in the dip.

PESTO-WRAPPED PRAWNS

BY HELENA LANG

SERVES 4 AS A STARTER

220 g unsmoked streaky bacon
5 tsp Sacla' Coriander Pesto
225 g cooked large king
    prawns, shelled
2½ tbsp olive oil
2 Little Gem lettuces, shredded
freshly ground black pepper
crusty Ciabatta bread, to serve

Helena Lang is Editor of Sainsbury's Magazine, *where she crafts each edition to appeal to busy working people who love to cook. This is a quick and simple recipe and works as a terrific starter.*

Lay the bacon on a chopping board and chop each rasher in half, vertically, so you are left with two strips, each approximately 8 cm long. Spread a teaspoon of Pesto along each strip. Wrap a piece of bacon around each prawn, with the Pesto in the middle, and secure with a cocktail stick.

Heat a tablespoon of oil in a frying pan over a medium heat and cook the bacon-wrapped prawns for a few minutes, until the bacon starts to turn golden.

Tip out onto a plate lined with kitchen paper to drain. Put the shredded lettuce on a serving plate and arrange the prawns on top. Mix a teaspoon of Pesto with the rest of the oil and drizzle over the prawns. Season with a little pepper and serve with some crusty Ciabatta.

PESTO PITTA CHIPS SERVES 4

3 tbsp olive oil

3 tbsp Sacla' Classic Basil Pesto

250 g pitta breads, split in half and each half cut into about 6 rough triangles

Preheat the oven to 200°C/400°F/gas 6. Place a baking tray in the oven to get nice and hot.

In a large bowl, mix together the oil and Pesto. Toss the pitta breads in the Pesto oil until they are thoroughly coated. Tip them onto the preheated baking tray and cook in the oven for about 10 minutes until crisp, turning once. Serve with Pesto Hummus or Chilli Pesto Soured Cream Dip (see pages 10 and 14).

AUBERGINE PESTO, BLACK OLIVE AND BASIL DIP SERVES 4

BY LORNA WING

380 g Sacla' Char-Grilled Aubergine Pesto

100g feta or Parmesan, crumbled into largish pieces

100g stoned black olives, roughly chopped

1 handful fresh basil leaves, torn into large pieces

chunky grissini or crudités, to dip

Lorna Wing is described as 'the peerless expert on food and entertaining' and she says this oh-so-easy Italian dip takes no time at all to assemble and never fails to impress. It can be made up to 3 hours ahead of time and kept covered and chilled in the fridge until your guests arrive.

Spoon the Pesto into a shallow serving dish. Scatter over the crumbled feta or Parmesan, followed by the olives and basil. Serve alongside some grissini or crudités for dipping.

2

LAZY LUNCHES

PESTO BAKED BEANS on TOAST

SERVES 4–6

1½ tbsp olive oil
1 medium onion, finely chopped
2 garlic cloves, finely chopped
1 tsp smoked paprika
200 g tomato passata
1 heaped tbsp brown sugar
(dark muscovado is best)
2 x 400 g cans haricot beans,
drained and rinsed
½ vegetable stock cube
4 tbsp Sacla' Organic Tomato
or Fiery Chilli Pesto
2 thick slices buttered toast,
per person, to serve

Traditionally, baked beans are cooked for anything from 1½ hours to overnight. This is a speedy version that will be ready from start to finish in 40 minutes, and most of that time it sits in the oven unattended. The beans taste great the next day, too. Organic Tomato Pesto is perfect if you're making this for the kids, or try it with Sacla' Fiery Chilli Pesto for the grown-ups.

Heat the oven to 180°C/350°F/gas 4.

Heat the oil in a frying pan over a medium heat and fry the onion for 10 minutes, until softened and golden.

Throw in the garlic and fry for a minute then stir in the paprika and cook for another minute. Add the passata, sugar, beans, 200 ml water and the stock cube. Stir together then bring to a simmer, stir again then cover with a lid and transfer to the oven to cook for 30 minutes. Check the beans after 20 minutes and if they are drying out, add a splash more water. Remove from the oven, stir in the Pesto and serve on hot buttered toast.

CREAMY PESTO MUSHROOMS *ON* TOAST

SERVES 2

1 tbsp olive oil, plus extra
    for drizzling
200 g chestnut mushrooms,
    sliced
2–4 thick slices of bread
2 tbsp Sacla' Classic Basil
    Pesto
1½ tbsp mascarpone cheese
1 small garlic clove (optional)
salt and freshly ground
    black pepper
fresh basil leaves, to garnish

A super speedy and luxurious lunch that you can easily scale up or down depending on how many are eating. Try it at the weekend for a lazy brunch – sourdough or Ciabatta toast will add a touch of sophistication.

Heat the oil in a large frying pan over a medium-high heat. Once it's hot, throw in the mushrooms and fry for 4 to 5 minutes, stirring every now and then, until the mushrooms are soft and starting to brown. Meanwhile, start toasting your bread.

Lower the heat under the mushrooms right down and stir in the Pesto, then stir in the mascarpone. Season with a little salt and a good grinding of black pepper.

Drizzle your toast with a little oil, and, if you like garlic, rub it all over with the clove of garlic. Tip the mushrooms on top, scatter with basil leaves and serve.

FARFALLE WITH PEPPERS, OLIVES AND MELTING MOZZARELLA

SERVES 2

200 g Farfalle
130 g Sacla' Char-Grilled
   Peppers Antipasto, roughly
   chopped, plus 2 tbsp of
   the oil
50 g stoned olives, halved
4 tbsp Sacla' Organic Tomato
   Pesto
125 g ball of mozzarella
salt and freshly ground
   black pepper
1 handful fresh basil leaves,
   roughly torn, to garnish

Try this with Sacla' Fiery Chilli Pesto to add a kick to your day! For a fresher taste, mix in a few halved cherry tomatoes and a handful of roughly chopped rocket leaves. It is also great as a cold salad – just toss the hot pasta with the peppers and olives and then leave it to cool before stirring through the torn mozzarella and lots of fresh basil.

In a large pan of salted boiling water, cook the pasta according to the packet instructions. Drain well, reserving about 4 tablespoons of the cooking water.

Meanwhile, heat the oil from the peppers in a frying pan over a medium heat, add the peppers and olives and toss together. Cook for 2 to 3 minutes, until heated through.

Add the drained pasta to the peppers and olives along with the Pesto. Mix gently to combine. Season with a little salt and pepper, then tear over the mozzarella. Heat through for a minute, until the mozzarella starts to melt. Serve, scattered with the basil leaves.

PAN-FRIED HALLOUMI WITH TOMATOES, ONIONS AND CORIANDER

SERVES 6

160 g cherry tomatoes
1 medium red onion, cut into wedges
1½ tbsp olive oil, plus extra for frying
2 tsp balsamic vinegar
pinch of dried chilli flakes (optional)
200 g halloumi cheese, sliced into 1 cm-thick slices
1 tbsp Sacla' Coriander Pesto
rocket or fresh coriander, chopped to garnish

This quick and colourful dish is great for an impromptu brunch or lunch and impressive served as a special starter, too. Cook the halloumi quickly over a high heat to prevent it going rubbery.

Preheat the oven to 200°C/400°F/gas 6. Toss together the tomatoes, onion, oil, vinegar and chilli flakes, if using. Tip into a roasting tray and spread out to create a fairly even layer. Roast for 20 minutes, until softened and caramelised.

Heat a drizzle of oil in a large non-stick frying pan over a medium–high heat. Pat the halloumi slices dry with kitchen paper and fry for 1 to 2 minutes on each side, until golden and just softening in the middle (you may need to cook the halloumi in batches if your pan isn't big enough).

Pile the roasted veggies onto serving plates, top with halloumi slices and a good dollop of the Coriander Pesto. Garnish with rocket or chopped coriander.

GRILLED PROSCIUTTO WITH PESTO SCRAMBLED EGGS

SERVES 2

4 slices prosciutto ham
4 thick slices Ciabatta
4 large eggs
100 ml milk
large knob of butter, plus extra
    for the toast
2 heaped tbsp Sacla' Classic
    Basil Pesto
1 handful freshly grated
    Parmesan
salt and freshly ground
    black pepper
a few small fresh basil leaves
    or chopped fresh chives,
    to garnish

Heat a large non-stick frying pan over a medium heat. Fry the prosciutto for a couple of minutes on each side, like you would bacon, until it's crisp and golden at the edges. Transfer to a warm plate.

Get your Ciabatta toasting while you crack on with the eggs. Lightly beat the eggs and milk with some salt and pepper. Melt the butter in the same pan in which you cooked the prosciutto, and turn the heat to low–medium. Pour in the eggs and top with the Pesto. Once the eggs are just starting to set on the bottom, gently stir them with a spatula, rippling in the Pesto as you go. Don't stir too much – you want lovely billowy folds as opposed to tiny bits of scrambled eggs.

Butter the toasted Ciabatta, tip the eggs on top and shower with freshly grated Parmesan. Rest the crisp prosciutto on top of the eggs and serve with plenty of pepper and some basil leaves or chopped chives scattered over the top.

MINESTRONE *ALLA* GENOVESE

BY ANNA DEL CONTE

SERVES 6

150 g aubergine, cut into
  2 cm-cubes
150 g green beans, topped and
  tailed and broken into
  3 cm-pieces
1 x 400 g can borlotti beans
200 g potatoes, cut into 2 cm-
  cubes
200 g cabbage, very coarsely
  shredded
250 g sweet onions, thickly
  sliced
150 g courgettes, cut into
  2 cm-cubes
2 sticks celery, cut into
  2 cm-pieces
100 g flat mushrooms, cut into
  2 cm-pieces
4 ripe tomatoes, peeled and
  coarsely chopped
150 g small tubular pasta, such
  as Ditalini
4 tbsp Sacla' Classic Basil
  Pesto
salt and freshly ground
  black pepper
fresh Parmesan, grated,
  to serve

Anna del Conte is the doyenne of Italian food in the UK and a prolific writer and author of many books. Here is her translation of a recipe published in 1894 in La Cuciniera Genovese *by G. B. and Giovanni Ratto, a book still considered to be the best on traditional Ligurian cooking. Obviously, at that time the Pesto was not from a jar, but for a quick and easy take, unscrew a jar of Sacla' Classic Basil Pesto and you will have an equally delicious Minestrone alla Genovese.*

Fill a stockpot with 2 litres of water, add 1 tablespoon of salt and bring to the boil over a medium heat. Add all the vegetables and simmer very gently, covered, for 2½ to 3 hours. The longer you cook a minestrone, the better it will be. The vegetables will not break or become mushy during the cooking; they keep their shape perfectly.

The last thing to do is to throw in the pasta, but before you do that, check that there is enough liquid for it to cook. If not, add a ladleful or two of boiling water. Remember, however, that this is a very thick soup and the pasta should cook gently, contrary to the usual way of cooking pasta when it is served drained.

When the pasta is cooked, taste and check the seasoning. Add a good grinding of pepper and the Pesto. Mix together well and serve with plenty of Parmesan on the side. In the summer, when you can get the best vegetables, serve the minestrone at room temperature.

PESTO, CHEESE *AND* HAM TOASTIES

MAKES 4 TOASTIES

8 thick slices bread (sourdough works best), or 4 panini
4 tbsp Sacla' Classic Basil Pesto
100 g good melting cheese such as Provolone, Emmental or Cheddar, sliced
4 slices of Parma ham or other cooked ham
butter, for spreading

This is a great way to make Italian-style toasted sandwiches without the need for a special panini machine. The secret is to get the pan just hot enough, so that by the time the bread has toasted, the middle is melty and delicious. If it's too hot, the bread could burn before the middle is ready, so always keep the heat lower if you're not sure – it will just take a little longer this way. Pack a punch with Sacla' Fiery Chilli Pesto or try Sacla' Sun-Dried Tomato Pesto for something extra unctuous.

Spread one side of each slice of bread with Pesto. Layer the cheese and then the ham on 4 of the slices, then top with the remaining bread, Pesto-side down, to make 4 sandwiches. Spread the outside of the bread with a little butter.

Heat a large frying pan over a medium heat and cook the toasties for 4 to 5 minutes on one side, until the bread underneath is toasted, pressing down gently with a spatula so that they cook evenly. Flip the toasties over and cook on the other side for a few more minutes until the bread is toasted and the cheese has melted. (You may need to cook them one at a time or in batches, depending on the size of your pan.) Cut in half diagonally, and serve straight away.

3

LUNCH ON THE GO

PANZANELLA

SERVES 2 AS A SIDE DISH

100 g stale rustic bread, torn
    into pieces
250 g ripe tomatoes, roughly
    chopped
½ cucumber, chopped into
    2 cm-pieces
1 tsp capers, drained
1 small red onion, finely sliced
1 large handful fresh basil
    leaves, plus extra to garnish
1–2 tbsp extra virgin olive oil,
    plus extra for drizzling
1–2 tsp red wine vinegar
3 tbsp Sacla' Classic Basil
    Pesto
salt and freshly ground
    black pepper

This lovely Italian summer salad was originally created to make use of stale bread! Try to use really ripe and juicy tomatoes – a mix of red and gold tomatoes will look stunning. It makes a great packed lunch and also goes brilliantly with grilled fish or meat at a barbecue.

Throw all the ingredients into a large bowl, giving the tomatoes a good squeeze as you go to release some of their juice. Toss everything together and have a taste to make sure you've added enough oil and vinegar – you might even like to add a bit more Pesto. Set aside for 20 to 30 minutes to let the bread soak up all the juices. To serve, tear over some fresh basil leaves and drizzle with a little more oil.

CHICKEN *AND* PESTO RICE

SERVES 2 AS A LIGHT LUNCH

125 g cooked brown rice

1 roasted chicken breast, shredded

1 red pepper, seeded and chopped into 2 cm-pieces

4 sun-dried tomatoes from Sacla' Sun-Dried Tomato Antipasto, chopped into 2 cm-pieces

1 handful rocket, roughly chopped

2 heaped tbsp Sacla' Sun-Dried Tomato Pesto

Colourful and packed with flavour, this effortlessly simple dish is a great stand-by for packed lunches. It also makes a filling supper for one.

In a large bowl, toss together all the ingredients and mix well to combine. Serve straight away or pack into a lunch box to eat the next day. Easy!

COURGETTE, PEA AND PESTO FRITTATA

SERVES 2 AS A MAIN, 4 AS A SNACK

2 tbsp olive oil
2 courgettes (about 250 g),
    coarsely grated
4 spring onions, thinly sliced
125 g frozen peas, defrosted
3 tbsp Sacla' Classic Basil
    Pesto
6 large eggs
50 g fresh Parmesan, grated
salt and freshly ground
    black pepper

This simple Italian-style omelette is just as good straight from the grill as it is cooled to room temperature. It will keep well in the fridge for a day, so use leftovers in a packed lunch or make a rustic sandwich.

Heat the oil in an ovenproof frying pan over a medium–high heat, chuck in the courgettes and fry for about 7 minutes, until golden-brown in places and any liquid from the courgettes has evaporated. Throw in the spring onions and fry for a couple more minutes. Next, add the peas, lower the heat to low–medium, and stir in the Pesto. Lightly beat the eggs with salt and pepper and pour over the vegetables. Stir gently to create a marbled effect, then sprinkle over the Parmesan. Cook for about 8 minutes, until set at the edges and golden-brown underneath (you can check by lifting up one side of the frittata with a spatula and having a peek).

Meanwhile, preheat the grill to medium and finish off the frittata under the grill for a couple of minutes, until just firm, bubbling and golden on top. Carefully slide the frittata out of the pan onto a plate and serve in wedges, hot or cold.

A SIMPLE PASTA DRESSING

BY
HENRIETTA
GREEN

SERVES 2

200 g wide Fettuccine
1 tbsp Sacla' Classic Basil
   Pesto
125 ml extra virgin olive oil
grated zest and juice of
   ½ lemon
1 handful of stoned black
   olives, roughly chopped
2 garlic cloves, roughly
   chopped
6 sun-dried tomatoes, from
   Sacla' Sun-Dried Tomato
   Antipasto, drained and
   roughly chopped
6 artichoke hearts, from Sacla'
   Artichoke Antipasto, drained
   and roughly chopped
1 small chilli, halved
   lengthways, seeded and
   roughly chopped
1 bunch of fresh flat-leaf
   parsley, roughly chopped
salt and freshly ground
   black pepper
fresh Parmesan, grated,
   to serve

Henrietta Green is an enthusiastic campaigner for the very best of great British food. This recipe for a simple pasta dressing is made from ingredients found in any respectable food lover's kitchen.

In a large pan of salted boiling water, cook the pasta according to the packet instructions.

Meanwhile, in a bowl, mix together the Pesto, oil and lemon zest and juice. Stir in the olives, garlic, sun-dried tomatoes, artichoke hearts, chilli and parsley, and season with a pinch of salt and pepper. Pour over the drained pasta and sprinkle with some freshly grated Parmesan.

PRIMAVERA SALAD WITH PESTO CHICKEN

SERVES 2-3

200 g chicken breast mini
 fillets
10 cherry tomatoes, halved
2 tbsp Sacla' Classic Basil
 Pesto

for the salad

100 g fine green beans
100 g sugar snap peas
8 fresh asparagus spears,
 woody ends removed
100 g mixed frozen peas,
 broad beans and soya beans
1½ tbsp Sacla' Classic Basil
 Pesto
a squeeze of lemon juice
extra virgin olive oil, to drizzle
2 Little Gem lettuce hearts,
 cut into quarters
freshly ground black pepper

This vibrant salad makes a satisfying and healthy lunch, or you can serve it while the chicken is still warm for a light supper. It's great with the Pesto Croutons on page 98 – wrap these separately if you're having it as a packed lunch so they don't go soggy.

Preheat the oven to 200°C/400°F/gas 6. In a small baking dish, mix together the chicken, tomatoes and Pesto. Roast in the oven for 10 to 12 minutes, until the chicken is completely cooked through. Remove from the oven and leave to cool.

For the salad, bring a large pan of salted water to the boil. Add in all the green veg, bring back to the boil and cook for 2 minutes. Drain well then toss with the Pesto and lemon juice and season with pepper. Add a drizzle of oil if you think it needs it. Once the vegetables have cooled, mix through the lettuce and top with the Pesto chicken.

MEDITERRANEAN VEGETABLE SALAD

SERVES 2 AS A MAIN, 4 AS A SIDE DISH

2 large courgettes, cut into
   3 cm-chunks
2 red peppers, cut into 3 cm-
   chunks
1 aubergine, cut into 3 cm-
   chunks
1 red onion, thickly sliced
3 tbsp olive oil
4 tbsp Sacla' Wild Rocket Pesto
50 g wild rocket leaves
salt and freshly ground
   black pepper
Parmesan shavings, to serve

A quick colourful salad that is great served hot or cold – pack it for lunch or to take on a picnic. It also makes a good side dish, served warm with grilled meat.

Preheat the oven to 180°C/350°C/gas 4. In a large roasting tray, toss all the vegetables together with the oil and season with salt and pepper. Roast for 30 to 40 minutes, turning once or twice, until sweet and caramelised.

Remove from the oven and, while they're still hot, mix through the Pesto. If you're serving the vegetables warm then toss the rocket through now so it wilts slightly; if you plan to have it as a cold salad then wait until the veggies have cooled down before adding the rocket. Garnish with Parmesan shavings.

PEA, PESTO, FARRO and LEMON SALAD

BY LUCAS HOLLWEG

SERVES 2 AS A STARTER OR LUNCH

Lucas Hollweg can be relied on for something a bit unusual and this recipe illustrates that. His first book Good Things to Eat *is full of similarly inspirational ideas.*
This is a light first course, although the farro gives it heft. You can find farro in Italian delis (or the British equivalent, pearl spelt, in delis and health food shops), if both elude you, use pearl barley instead. It will just need longer to cook.

100 g uncooked pearl farro
 (or pearl spelt)
225 g sugar snap peas
125 g fresh podded peas
 (or frozen petit pois)
6 tbsp Sacla' Classic
 Basil Pesto
grated zest of 1 lemon,
 plus 1 tbsp of the juice
4 tbsp extra virgin olive oil
4 big handfuls of rocket
flaked sea salt and freshly
 ground black pepper
a few basil leaves, to garnish
Parmesan or Pecorino cheese
 shavings, to serve

Put the farro in a bowl, cover with cold water and leave to soak for 15 minutes. Carefully peel off and discard any stringy bits from the sides of the sugar snap peas.

Drain, then tip the farro into a saucepan. Cover with cold water and bring to the boil over a medium heat. Cook for 20 to 30 minutes, until the grains are soft. Go by texture rather than timing. Drain well and leave to cool. Wipe out the saucepan.

Put the saucepan back on the stove and bring plenty of salted water to the boil. Add the sugar snap and podded peas and cook for 2 to 3 minutes, until just cooked. Drain and quickly run under cold water for 30 seconds to stop them cooking and cool them down. Drain again, shaking off any water.

Put the Pesto in a mixing bowl, along with the lemon juice and 2 tablespoons of the oil. Add the drained farro, the sugar snap and podded peas, and stir until everything is combined. Loosely toss in the rocket. Season, to taste, with salt and pepper, then divide the salad between bowls. Drizzle with the rest of the oil and tear a few basil leaves over the top. Scatter with the lemon zest, plus a few shavings of Parmesan or Pecorino, then finish with a grind of black pepper.

FRESH TROFIE *WITH* FRESH TOMATO SAUCE

SERVES 2

300 g Sacla' Trofie pasta
3 large, ripe tomatoes,
    roughly chopped
1 handful of fresh basil leaves,
    roughly torn, plus extra
    to garnish
3 tbsp extra virgin olive oil,
    plus extra to drizzle
150 g Sacla' Classic Basil Pesto
salt and freshly ground
    black pepper

This dish tastes great cold, once the pasta has had a chance to soak up all the lovely flavours of the Pesto, ripe tomatoes and extra virgin olive oil. You can also eat it straight away – the hot pasta and cold tomatoes provide a surprisingly satisfying sensation.

In a large pan of salted boiling water, cook the pasta according to the packet instructions. Drain well, then immediately toss the pasta with the tomatoes, basil, oil and Pesto. Season with salt and pepper. Serve with more torn basil scattered over the top and a good drizzle of oil.

4

FIRE UP THE GRILL

HOMEMADE LAMB BURGERS MAKES 4 BURGERS

1 small red onion, cut into
    quarters
2 garlic cloves
400 g minced lamb (not too
    lean, about 20 per cent fat
    is best)
3 tbsp Sacla' Classic Basil
    Pesto
1 handful fresh mint leaves
    (optional)
salt and freshly ground
    black pepper
toasted burger buns, rocket
    and tomato slices, to serve

Put the onion and garlic into a food processor and blitz until roughly chopped. Add the lamb, Pesto, mint, if using, and a generous amount of salt and pepper. Pulse until just combined. Be careful not to over process – you want to keep some texture (alternatively, you can do it all by hand: just finely chop or grate the red onion and garlic and mix everything together).

Divide the mixture into four and shape into burgers. If you have time, pop them on a plate and chill them in the fridge for half an hour before cooking. You can even do this stage the day before and keep them in the fridge overnight.

Fire up the barbecue or preheat a griddle pan or the grill, and cook the burgers for 4 to 5 minutes on each side, until nicely browned and cooked through.

Serve in toasted burger buns with a handful of rocket and some sliced tomatoes.

BARBECUED CORN ON THE COB SERVES 4 AS A SNACK OR SIDE

4 cobs of corn
olive oil, for brushing
75 g Sacla' Fiery Chilli Pesto
salt

Heat up the barbecue so it's nice and hot (or you can use a griddle pan indoors).

Bring a large pan of salted water to the boil and cook the corn cobs for 10 minutes, until they are just tender but not completely cooked through. Drain well then brush with a little oil. Barbecue or griddle the corn for 5 to 10 minutes, depending on the heat, turning occasionally, until charred in places.

Tip the Pesto into a shallow dish and roll the hot corn cobs in the Pesto to cover them all over.

CHAR-GRILLED STEAK
WITH PESTO 'CAESAR' SALAD

SERVES 4

4 rib-eye or sirloin steaks
olive oil, to drizzle
1 Cos or Romaine lettuce, or
   4 Little Gem hearts,
   roughly torn
1 handful of Pesto Croutons
   (see page 98)
flaked sea salt

for the 'Caesar' dressing

4 tbsp mayonnaise
4 tbsp soured cream
2 tbsp Sacla' Classic Basil
   Pesto
1½ tsp lemon juice
25 g fresh Parmesan, grated
1 small garlic clove, crushed
salt and freshly ground
   black pepper

Whisk all of the dressing ingredients together in a small bowl, and season with salt and pepper, to taste.

Preheat a griddle pan or large frying pan over a high heat. Rub the steaks on both sides with a little oil and season with flaked sea salt. Once the pan is really hot, fry the steaks for 3 to 4 minutes on each side for medium-rare, or until cooked to your liking (don't overcrowd the pan or you won't get that lovely brown crust – you might need to cook them in two batches). Leave the steaks to rest on a board for a couple of minutes while you assemble the salad.

Toss the lettuce with enough of the dressing to lightly coat the leaves then divide between serving bowls. Scatter over some croutons. Cut the steaks into thick slices and arrange on top of the salad. Serve straight away.

BUTTERFLIED PESTO CHICKEN
WITH MOZZARELLA SALAD

SERVES 4

4 chicken breasts, skin removed

150 g Sacla' Sun-Dried Tomato Pesto

2 tbsp extra virgin olive oil, plus extra for drizzling

240 g baby buffalo mozzarella balls

250 g baby plum tomatoes, halved lengthways, to serve

rocket, to serve

This is a casual, no-fuss dish, perfect for easy lunches or eating al fresco. If you want to make it a bit more elegant, or turn it into fork-only food, carve the chicken diagonally into slices and scatter on top of the salad.

Using a sharp knife, butterfly each chicken breast by cutting it almost in half horizontally, so that it opens up into one large, thin breast. Score a few diagonal lines on both sides then rub all over with half the Pesto and the oil. Set aside to marinate for a few minutes while you fire up the barbecue or preheat a griddle pan or the grill. Cook the chicken for 3 to 4 minutes on each side, until just charred in places and the chicken is cooked through.

Meanwhile, toss the mozzarella balls with the rest of the Pesto.

Arrange the tomatoes and rocket on serving plates, then scatter over the mozzarella balls. Top with the hot chicken, drizzle with a little oil and serve.

GRILLED SHELLFISH GAZPACHO

BY ANTONY WORRALL THOMPSON

SERVES 4

1 slice wholegrain country
  bread, crusts removed and
  broken into small chunks
2 tsp sherry vinegar
½ garlic clove, finely chopped
1 tsp caster sugar
½ red chilli, halved
  lengthways, seeded and
  finely diced
2 tbsp extra virgin olive oil,
  plus extra to grill the
  seafood
225 g Sacla' Sun-Dried Tomato
  Antipasto, drained, or 190 g
  Sacla' Sun-Dried Tomato
  Pesto
200 ml tomato juice
2 spring onions, finely sliced
½ pepper, roasted
¼ large cucumber, peeled,
  seeded and roughly diced
2 tsp Sacla' Classic Basil Pesto
4 raw large prawns, shelled
4 scallops, shucked
juice of ½ a lemon
salt and freshly ground
  black pepper
1 handful chopped fresh basil
  leaves, to serve
125 g white crabmeat, to serve

Antony Worrall Thompson is something of a legend – a prolific writer and broadcaster, a fantastic restaurateur and a businessman. Inspired by his house in Spain, this dish combines delicious Spanish flavours with the freshness of seafood.

Place the bread in a food processor or blender. With the machine running, add the vinegar, garlic, sugar and chilli, and blend until smooth. Add the oil, a little at a time, until absorbed by the bread. Add the Sun-Dried Tomato (Antipasto or Pesto), tomato juice, spring onions, roasted pepper, cucumber and Basil Pesto. Continue to blend to form a smooth emulsion. Season with salt and pepper, to taste. Chill in the fridge until ready to serve.

Just before serving, preheat the grill or a griddle or heavy-based frying pan over a high heat. Season the prawns and scallops with lemon juice and pepper. Brush with a little oil and cook for 1½ minutes, until the prawns are opaque and a lovely pink colour.

Ideally, serve this soup in large-rimmed shallow bowls. Arrange the prawns and scallops in the centre of each bowl and pour the soup around the shellfish. Scatter each bowl with chopped basil leaves and fresh crab, and serve immediately.

FISH PARCELS *WITH* GREEN POTATO SALAD

SERVES 4

120 g Sacla' Char-Grilled
    Peppers Antipasto, plus
    4 tsp of the oil and extra
    for greasing
4 x 100 g sea bass fillets
1 handful fresh basil leaves
pinch of dried chilli flakes
salt and freshly ground
    black pepper

for the green potato salad

600 g waxy new potatoes
150 g frozen peas
150 g frozen broad beans
100 g Sacla' Classic Basil Pesto
juice of ½ a lemon
1 tbsp extra virgin olive oil
2 tbsp finely chopped fresh
    chives
2 tbsp finely chopped fresh
    flat-leaf parsley leaves
4 tbsp mayonnaise

Easy yet elegant, this is fab cooked on the barbecue but it also works well in the oven if it's a bit chilly outside!

For the green potato salad, boil the potatoes in a large pan of salted water for 15 to 20 minutes, until tender. Throw in the peas and beans for the last 3 minutes of cooking. Drain well and, while still warm so they absorb all the delicious flavours, cut the potatoes in half and toss with the peas and beans in the Pesto, lemon juice and oil. Once cool, mix in the herbs and mayonnaise. Set aside until ready to serve.

For the fish, fire up the barbecue or preheat the oven to 200°C/400°F/gas 6.

Tear off four sheets of foil, each big enough to wrap generously around a fish fillet. Spread a little of the oil from the peppers in the middle of each piece of foil, then place a sea bass fillet on top, skin-side down. Scatter the peppers over the fish followed by the basil, chilli and a little salt and pepper. Drizzle with a teaspoon of oil from the peppers. Bring the foil loosely up around the fish and fold it over to seal it tightly in the middle. They should look a bit like giant silver Cornish pasties. Cook the parcels on the barbecue or on a baking tray in the oven for 10 to 12 minutes, depending on the thickness of the fish. Serve in their foil, unwrapping carefully as the steam escapes, with a generous mound of the potato salad on the side.

5

SOMETHING SPECIAL

PIEMONTESE PEPPERS WITH PESTO

SERVES 4

4 large red peppers, halved
    and seeded
4 tomatoes, cut into quarters
3 garlic cloves, finely sliced
4 tbsp Sacla' Classic Basil
    Pesto
5 tbsp olive oil
salt and freshly ground
    black pepper
1 small handful fresh basil
    leaves, to garnish

Pesto replaces the traditional anchovy in this classic dish. The Pesto and olive oil cook together slowly with the sweet peppers, creating lots of lovely juices to soak up with hunks of crusty bread. Serve the peppers warm or cold, for an al fresco lunch or as a delicious antipasti. For a decorative twist, leave the stalks on the peppers.

Preheat the oven to 180°C/350°F/gas 4.

Arrange the peppers cut-side up in a baking dish. Tuck the tomato pieces inside the cavities of the peppers along with the garlic. Spoon in the Pesto, then drizzle with the oil. Season with salt and pepper and roast for 45 minutes, until the peppers are soft and tender and very slightly golden at the edges – be careful not to let them burn (lower the heat if they look like they might be cooking too quickly). When ready to serve, spoon over the juices and scatter with fresh basil leaves.

CHICKEN *with* A PARMESAN *and* PESTO CRUST

SERVES 4

olive oil, for greasing and
   drizzling
4 chicken breasts, skin
   removed
100 g fresh breadcrumbs
45 g fresh Parmesan, grated
45 g pine nuts
3 tbsp chopped fresh parsley
4–5 tbsp Sacla' Classic Basil
   Pesto
salt and freshly ground
   black pepper

Toasted pine nuts add a tasty crunch to an everyday chicken breast. Serve this alongside some steamed green vegetables or a salad, and some creamy mashed potatoes.

Preheat the oven to 200°C/400°F/gas 6. Lightly grease a baking tray with a little oil.

Slice each chicken breast in half horizontally, to make eight thin fillets.

In a small bowl mix together the breadcrumbs, Parmesan, pine nuts and parsley, and season with salt and pepper. Spread the Pesto all over the chicken breasts then cover generously with the cheesy crumb mixture. Place on the baking tray and scatter over any remaining topping. Drizzle with a little oil and cook for 15 to 20 minutes, until the crumbs are golden and the chicken is cooked through.

BAKED PAPPARDELLE *WITH* PESTO, PORCINI *AND* PANCETTA

SERVES 2

25 g dried porcini mushrooms
250 ml boiling water
200 g Pappardelle
100 g pancetta cubes
150 g mascarpone cheese
2 tbsp Sacla' Classic Basil
    Pesto
40 g fresh Parmesan, grated
salt and freshly ground
    black pepper

Creamy and indulgent yet so quick to prepare, this is an elegant meal for two. Serve with a crisp green salad dressed with a little olive oil and balsamic vinegar.

Preheat the oven to 200°C/400°F/gas 6.

Put the porcini in a small bowl and cover with the boiling water. Leave to soak for 10 minutes. Drain, reserving the soaking liquid, and roughly chop.

In a large pan of salted boiling water, cook the pasta according to the packet instructions. Drain well, reserving a few spoonfuls of the cooking water.

Heat a frying pan over a medium heat and fry the pancetta for about 4 minutes, until lightly golden. Pour away most of the fat, leaving just enough to fry the mushrooms. Turn the heat to low, stir in the porcini and fry for a minute. Pour in most of the porcini soaking water, being careful to leave behind the last few spoonfuls, which may be gritty. Bubble for 1 to 2 minutes, until the liquid has reduced slightly. Stir in the mascarpone and Pesto, and heat through, stirring gently, for a couple of minutes. Add about 5 tablespoons of the pasta cooking water to loosen the sauce, season with salt and pepper and mix in the drained pasta. Tip into a baking dish, sprinkle with the Parmesan and bake for 10 minutes, until golden.

RISOTTO WITH PRAWNS AND PESTO

SERVES 2–3

1.2 litres vegetable or light
  fish stock
a knob of butter
2 tbsp olive oil
1 small onion, finely chopped
300 g Arborio rice
100 ml white wine
150 g frozen peas, defrosted
200 g raw king prawns, shelled
grated zest of 1 lemon
100 g Sacla' Classic Basil Pesto
1 tbsp chopped fresh parsley or
  1 handful chopped rocket
1 handful freshly grated
  Parmesan
salt and freshly ground
  black pepper

Bring the stock to the boil in a small saucepan, then turn down the heat to low and keep it at a very gentle simmer.

In a large saucepan, heat the butter and oil over a medium heat. Add the onion and fry gently for about 5 minutes, until soft and lightly golden.

Tip in the rice and stir for a minute to coat in the buttery onion, then pour in the white wine. Let it bubble, then give it a good stir and add a couple of ladlefuls of hot stock, stirring all the time. Add the rest of the stock, a couple of ladlefuls at a time, keeping back about one ladleful. Stir between each addition until the liquid is almost completely absorbed, before adding the next – this part will take about 20 minutes. You don't have to stir constantly, but the more you stir, the creamier the risotto will be.

Add the peas and prawns and the reserved ladleful of stock, and cook for 5 minutes until the prawns turn pink and are cooked through. To check the rice is cooked, taste a few grains; it should be soft but with a slight bite. If it needs a bit longer, add a little hot water. Stir in the lemon zest, Pesto, parsley or rocket, salt and pepper and most of the Parmesan, and mix together well. Cover the pan and leave to rest for a minute then serve with the rest of the Parmesan and lots of black pepper.

PESTO AND MASCARPONE-STUFFED CHICKEN BREASTS

SERVES 2

olive oil, to drizzle
2 chicken breasts, skin
    removed
100 g mascarpone cheese
2 tbsp Sacla' Classic Basil
    Pesto
1 tbsp finely chopped fresh
    chives or flat-leaf parsley,
    plus extra to garnish
6 slices Parma ham
50 ml hot chicken stock
salt and freshly ground
    black pepper

The mascarpone and Pesto keep the chicken juicy and moist and mingle with the chicken juices during cooking to make a delicious dish. Serve with fine green beans or a rocket salad and some sautéed potatoes.

Preheat the oven to 220°C/425°F/gas 7. Lightly oil a small roasting tray. Using a sharp knife cut a pocket into the side of each chicken breast, being careful not to cut through to the other side.

Mix together the mascarpone, Pesto, herbs and some salt and use this to stuff the chicken breasts. Don't worry if some of the filling spills out; rub this over the outside of the chicken to keep it extra moist and juicy.

Season the chicken breasts with pepper then wrap them in the slices of Parma ham, making sure you seal the pocket (don't wrap them up too tightly, though, as this can cause the filling to ooze out during cooking). Arrange the chicken parcels in the roasting tray and cook in the oven for 10 minutes. Lower the heat to 200°C/400°F/gas 6, pour over the hot stock and cook for 15 minutes, until the chicken is cooked through. Serve the chicken on warm plates and spoon over any excess sauce from the tray. Garnish with fresh herbs.

TASTY TOMATO PESTO-STUFFED VINE LEAVES

BY PHIL VICKERY

SERVES 6–8

Phil Vickery's delicious and interesting recipes have placed him as one of Britain's favourite chefs. Phil says, 'when cooked properly, stuffed vine leaves are one of my favourites. In this recipe I have added a twist by using a jar of Sacla' Sun-Dried Tomato Pesto'.

225 g long grain rice
6 tbsp olive oil
1 small onion, finely chopped
2 garlic cloves, crushed
3 tbsp chopped fresh basil leaves
3 tbsp chopped fresh mint leaves
190 g Sacla' Sun-Dried Tomato Pesto
12–15 vine leaves, soaked in boiling water for a few minutes, then rinsed well
500 ml hot vegetable or chicken stock
juice of 1 lemon
salt

In a large pan of salted boiling water, cook the rice for half the time recommended on the packet instructions. Drain and refresh by running under cold water, then drain well.

Preheat the oven to 200°C/400°F/gas 6.

Heat the oil in a frying pan over a medium heat and cook the onion and garlic for 3 minutes. Spoon into a bowl and add the rice. Mix together well. Add the basil, mint and Pesto and mix well again.

Lay a vine leaf on a flat surface and place a spoonful of the rice mixture in the middle of the leaf. Fold over the sides of the leaf to make a little parcel. Repeat with the rest of the rice mixture.

Pack the stuffed vine leaves quite tightly into a shallow, ovenproof saucepan. Pour over enough hot stock just to cover the vine leaves (you may not need to use it all). Add the lemon juice.

Heat the saucepan over a medium heat until the stock is simmering gently. Place an ovenproof plate on top of the stuffed vine leaves and cover with the lid. Cook in the oven for 35 minutes, until the vine leaves are plump and full and they have absorbed all the stock. Drizzle with a little oil and leave to cool for 10 minutes before serving.

PESTO ROAST POTATOES

SERVES 4

1 kg potatoes, cut into 4 cm-chunks

3 tbsp olive oil

2 tbsp polenta

100 g Sacla' Classic Basil Pesto

3 rosemary sprigs, leaves picked

1 garlic bulb, separated into cloves, unpeeled

Preheat the oven to 200°C/400°F/gas 6.

Put the potatoes in a large saucepan of cold water, bring to the boil and cook for 6 minutes, until just tender. Pour the oil into a large roasting tray and pop it into the oven to heat up.

Drain the potatoes well, leave them to steam dry for a minute in the colander, then tip them back into the saucepan. Add the polenta, put the lid on the pan and give them a really good shake to bash them about and rough up the edges. Spoon in the Pesto and give them another, slightly more gentle shake.

Carefully arrange the potatoes in the hot oil and scatter with the rosemary and garlic. Roast for about 50 minutes, turning once, until crisp and golden.

PESTO *AND* TOMATO TART

SERVES 4

1 x 320 g packet ready-rolled
   puff pastry
3 tbsp Sacla' Classic Basil
   Pesto
100 g crumbly goats' cheese
250 g cherry tomatoes
2 tbsp olive oil
1 tsp sugar
salt and freshly ground
   black pepper
1 handful of fresh basil leaves
   or rocket, to garnish

Preheat the oven to 220°C/425°F/gas 7.

Place the pastry on a baking tray then score a
2 cm-border all the way round the edge – this will
rise to form a crust.

Spread the Pesto over the pastry inside the border
and crumble over the goats' cheese.

Cut the tomatoes into halves, or quarters if they're
very plump, and toss in the oil, sugar and a little
salt and pepper. Scatter them on top of the goats'
cheese, turning most of them cut-side up – but don't
be too much of a perfectionist about it! Cook in the
oven for 20 minutes, until the pastry has puffed up
and is golden at the edges. Scatter with fresh basil
leaves or rocket and serve.

CONCHIGLIE *WITH* CHICKEN, CREAMY PESTO *AND* PEAS

SERVES 2

200 g Sacla' Conchiglie pasta

125 g frozen peas

1 tbsp olive oil

150 g chicken mini fillets, or chicken breast, cut into long, thin strips

100 ml double cream

4 tbsp Sacla' Classic Basil Pesto

2 tbsp freshly grated Parmesan, plus extra to serve

salt and freshly ground black pepper

a few fresh basil leaves, to garnish

You can create lots of variations of this dish, depending on what you have to hand. For extra richness, add some cubed pancetta or smoked bacon to the pan with the chicken, or substitute some or all of the peas with asparagus tips, green beans or broad beans for a lighter, fresher meal.

In a large pan of salted boiling water, cook the pasta according to the packet instructions. Add the peas for the last 2 minutes of cooking time. Drain well, reserving a few spoonfuls of the cooking water.

In a large frying pan heat the oil over a high heat. Season the chicken fillets with salt and pepper, and fry them for 2 to 3 minutes, until browned and cooked through.

Turn the heat down to low then pour in the cream. Stir the cream as it bubbles to pick up any of the browned bits from the bottom of the pan, then stir in the Pesto.

Add the pasta and peas and a few spoonfuls of the cooking water to make a silky, creamy sauce. Stir in the Parmesan, check and adjust the seasoning, and add a little more cooking water if needed. Serve in warm pasta bowls, topped with basil leaves, freshly ground black pepper and some more Parmesan.

PESTO, GOATS' CHEESE
AND ROCKET LINGUINE

SERVES 2

200 g Linguine
150 g Sacla' Classic Basil Pesto
100 g goats' cheese
50 g rocket, roughly chopped
grated zest of 1 lemon
extra virgin olive oil, to drizzle
salt and freshly ground
   black pepper

In a large pan of salted boiling water, cook the pasta according to the packet instructions. Drain well, then return the pasta to the hot pan.

Mix in the Pesto, then crumble in the goats' cheese and stir to combine. Add the rocket, lemon zest and lots of black pepper and toss together. Serve drizzled with a little oil.

PAN-FRIED LAMB STEAKS *WITH* A QUICK BUTTERBEAN MASH

SERVES 4

4 lamb leg steaks
olive oil, to drizzle

for the Pesto butter

50 g butter, softened
25 g Sacla' Sun-Dried Tomato Antipasto, finely chopped
1 tbsp Sacla' Classic Basil Pesto
1 heaped tbsp chopped fresh basil leaves

for the quick butterbean mash

2 x 400 g cans butterbeans, drained and rinsed
1 tbsp olive oil
1 vegetable stock cube
100 ml boiling water
2 tbsp Sacla' Classic Basil Pesto

This is a surprisingly light dish – perfect for a special occasion. Serve with green beans or a simple salad.

First make the Pesto butter by mixing all the ingredients together in a small bowl until well blended. Spoon the mixture into a rough sausage shape on a piece of greaseproof paper. Chill in the fridge for about 30 minutes, until it has firmed up a little and then roll into a neater sausage-shape. Chill until needed.

To make the mash, put the beans, oil, stock cube and boiling water in a small saucepan. Warm through over a medium heat then remove from the heat and blend to a smooth purée using a stick blender (or mash by hand for a rougher texture). Stir in the Pesto. Set aside and keep warm while you prepare the steaks.

Drizzle the steaks with a little oil. Heat a griddle pan over a high heat. Cook the steaks for 2 to 3 minutes on each side, depending on the thickness, until nicely browned on the outside and cooked to your liking. Serve the steaks on a mound of the butterbean mash, topped with a couple of slices of the Pesto butter.

FILLET STEAK *WITH* A PESTO PINE NUT CRUST *AND* BALSAMIC ONIONS

SERVES 2

2 x 150 g fillet steaks
olive oil, to drizzle

for the Pesto pine nut crust

2 tbsp pine nuts, toasted and
    roughly chopped
2 tbsp fresh breadcrumbs
1 tbsp freshly grated Parmesan
1 tbsp Sacla' Classic Basil
    Pesto
1 tbsp finely chopped fresh
    parsley
salt and freshly ground
    black pepper

for the balsamic onions

1 tbsp olive oil
a knob of butter
1 large red onion, sliced
1 tbsp balsamic vinegar

You can fry the steaks and add the topping an hour in advance, then just pop them in the preheated oven when you're nearly ready to eat. The sweet richness of the onions and the crust works really well served alongside some blanched green beans and little sautéed potatoes.

First prepare the balsamic onions. In a heavy-based saucepan heat the oil and butter over a medium heat. Add the onion and cook for 15 to 20 minutes, stirring occasionally, until softened and golden. Pour in the vinegar and simmer for 5 minutes, until reduced to a sticky glaze. Set aside and keep warm.

Preheat the oven to 220°C/425°F/gas 7. In a small bowl, mix together all the ingredients for the Pesto pine nut crust.

Heat a frying pan over a medium–high heat. Rub the steaks with a little oil. When the pan is really hot add the steaks and fry, without moving them, for a minute on each side, so they get a nice brown crust. Remove from the pan and transfer to a roasting tray.

Pile the crust mixture on top of each steak and cook in the oven for 3 to 4 minutes for rare, 4 to 5 minutes for medium. Leave to rest for a couple of minutes before serving alongside the balsamic onions.

ORECCHIETTE *CON* MELANZANE *E* POMODORI

BY THEO RANDALL

SERVES 4 AS A STARTER

3 tbsp olive oil
1 garlic clove, finely sliced
5 fresh basil leaves
1 x 400 g can chopped tomatoes
190 g Sacla' Char-Grilled
    Aubergine Pesto
300 g Sacla' Orecchiette pasta
salt and freshly ground
    black pepper
80 g fresh Parmesan, grated,
    to serve

Theo Randall gained his first Michelin Star at the renowned River Café and in London he continues to specialise in Italian cuisine at his restaurant. Theo says, 'I love this pasta dish because it is really healthy fast food. The combination of tomatoes and creamy aubergine is delicious. With the addition of fresh basil and olive oil you can almost feel the sun!'

Heat 2 tablespoons of the oil in a large non-stick frying pan over a medium heat. Add the garlic and 3 of the basil leaves and cook for 30 seconds. Pour in the tomatoes and cook gently for about 10 minutes, until the tomatoes have reduced by half. Stir in the Pesto, cook for a couple of minutes and then season with salt and pepper.

In a large pan of salted boiling water cook the pasta according to the packet instructions. Using a slotted spoon, lift the pasta directly into the pan with the sauce. Drizzle with the rest of the oil and tear over the remaining basil leaves. Add a tablespoon or two of the pasta cooking water and toss thoroughly, until the pasta is fully coated in the sauce.

Give the seasoning a final check, and serve with plenty of Parmesan and a glass of Primitivo di Puglia!

6

WINTER WARMERS

CARROT SOUP *WITH* CORIANDER PESTO

SERVES 4

1 tbsp olive oil
1 onion, roughly chopped
500 g carrots, peeled and
   roughly chopped
1 tsp ground coriander
750 ml–1 litre vegetable or
   chicken stock
4 tsp Sacla' Coriander Pesto
salt and freshly ground
   black pepper

Super healthy, vibrant and very easy to make, this is a lovely warming soup for cosy suppers or weekday lunches. It also freezes well. Reheat gently and swirl through some Sacla' Coriander Pesto for a fab colour contrast.

Heat the oil in a large saucepan over a medium heat. Add the onion and cook gently for about 5 minutes, until softened and just starting to turn golden. Stir in the carrots and ground coriander and cook for a minute. Pour in 750 ml of the stock and bring to the boil. Lower the heat and simmer, partly covered with a lid, for 30 to 40 minutes, until the carrots are lovely and tender.

Using a stick blender, purée the soup, adding a little extra hot stock if needed until you get the consistency you like. Season, to taste, with salt and pepper. Ladle into warm bowls and swirl a dollop of Pesto on top, followed by a good grinding of black pepper.

ROASTED TOMATO SOUP
WITH PESTO CROUTONS SERVES 4

1 kg ripe tomatoes, halved or
    cut into quarters if plump
2 carrots, peeled and roughly
    chopped
2 large red onions, roughly
    chopped
2 plump garlic cloves
4 tbsp olive oil
750 ml–1 litre hot chicken or
    vegetable stock
pinch of sugar
salt and freshly ground
    black pepper
2 tbsp mascarpone cheese,
    to serve
a few fresh basil leaves,
    to garnish

for the Pesto croutons

3–4 slices bread (about 100 g)
2 tbsp Sacla' Classic Basil
    Pesto
2 tbsp olive oil
flaked sea salt

Roasting the tomatoes with red onions and carrots brings maximum sweetness and flavour to this warming soup. For a real whack of tomato flavour, stir a spoonful or two of Sacla' Sun-Dried Tomato Pesto into the soup just before serving. If you don't fancy making the croutons, replace them with a swirl of Sacla' Classic Basil Pesto.

Preheat the oven to 200°C/400°F/gas 6. Tip the tomatoes, carrot, red onion and garlic into a roasting tray. Toss with the oil and season with salt and pepper. Roast for 45 minutes, until soft and golden in places.

While they're roasting, whip up the croutons. Tear the bread into rough bite-sized pieces, spread them out onto a baking tray and mix thoroughly with the Pesto, oil and a generous pinch of salt. Put them in the oven, on the shelf above the veg, and cook for 8 to 10 minutes, stirring once, until crisp and toasty (timings may vary depending on what type of bread you use). Remove from the oven and set aside. (Stored in an airtight container, the croutons will stay crunchy for up to 4 days. If they go a little soggy, just pop them in a hot oven for a few minutes to crisp up.)

When the vegetables are soft and golden, scrape them into a large saucepan along with any lovely caramelized sticky bits from the bottom of the roasting tray. Add 750 ml of hot stock and heat gently over a medium heat. Simmer for 15 minutes and then, using a stick blender, purée the soup, adding a little extra hot stock if needed until you get the consistency you like. Season, to taste, with salt, pepper and a pinch of sugar. Give it a good stir, then ladle into warm bowls and top with a swirl of mascarpone and a handful of crunchy Pesto croutons. Garnish with a few basil leaves.

POTATO *AND* PESTO GRATIN

SERVES 4 AS A SIDE DISH

1 kg potatoes, peeled and
    thinly sliced
olive oil, for greasing
4 tbsp Sacla' Classic Basil
    Pesto
500 ml milk
150 g mascarpone cheese
1 handful of freshly grated
    Parmesan
salt and freshly ground
    black pepper

This creamy and indulgent dish makes a delicious supper, served with a crunchy green salad. Or try it alongside roast chicken for the ultimate Sunday lunch. Slice the potatoes as thinly as you can (a mandolin or food processor slicing attachment will make this easier).

Preheat the oven to 160°C/325°F/gas 3. Pat the potato slices dry with a tea towel.

Grease a 20 cm x 30 cm baking dish with a little oil. Arrange half the potatoes in a couple of layers in the dish, and top with half the Pesto – try to spread the Pesto as evenly as you can over the potatoes. Season with salt and pepper and top with the rest of the potatoes and the remaining Pesto.

Mix together the milk and mascarpone (don't worry if it's a little lumpy, it will smooth out during cooking) and pour this over the potatoes. Season with a little salt and pepper, and sprinkle over the Parmesan. Place on a baking tray (to catch any drips as it cooks), and bake in the oven for 1½ hours, until the potatoes are tender (if the top starts to darken too quickly cover loosely with foil). Leave to rest for 10 minutes before serving.

TUNA AND PESTO PASTA BAKE

SERVES 4–6

400 g Sacla' Conchiglie pasta
300 g frozen peas
2 x 185 g cans tuna in brine,
    drained
190 g Sacla' Classic Basil Pesto
1 small red onion, finely
    chopped

for the cheese sauce

75 g plain flour
75 g butter
900 ml–1 litre milk
100 g Cheddar, grated
25 g fresh Parmesan, grated
salt and freshly ground
    black pepper

*Cosy comfort food that all the family will love.
Best served straight from the oven while the cheesy
topping is still bubbling.*

Preheat the oven to 200°C/400°F/gas 6.

In a large pan of salted boiling water, cook the pasta
according to the packet instructions. Add the peas for
the last 2 minutes of cooking time. Drain well, then
return to the hot pan and mix together with the tuna,
Pesto and onion.

While the pasta is cooking, you can make a start on
the cheese sauce. Tip the flour, butter and 900 ml milk
into a large saucepan. Place over a medium heat and
stir continuously with a balloon whisk for 5 to 10
minutes, until the butter has melted and the sauce
starts to bubble. At this point, lower the heat right
down and simmer for 5 minutes, stirring occasionally.
Season with salt and pepper, then remove from the
heat and stir in most of the Cheddar, reserving some
for the topping. You want the sauce to be the
consistency of double cream, so add a little more
milk if needed.

Gently stir the sauce into the pasta mixture until well
combined. Tip into a large ovenproof dish and scatter
with the remaining Cheddar and the Parmesan. Place
on a baking tray (to catch any drips as it cooks), and
bake in the oven for 20 to 25 minutes until golden
and bubbling.

ITALIAN LAMB RAGÙ
WITH FRESH PASTA

BY DHRUV BAKER

SERVES 6

1 tbsp olive oil
800 g lamb neck fillets
2 onions, finely chopped
4 garlic cloves, finely chopped
125 ml dry white wine
185 g Sacla' Spicy Roasted
   Pepper Pesto
500 ml hot fresh chicken stock
a few sprigs of fresh thyme
600 g Sacla' Trofie pasta
salt and freshly ground
   black pepper

This is a maestro recipe from Dhruv Baker, the MasterChef Winner of 2010. There are lots of Dhruv's recipes on the Sacla' website, but here's his own favourite of Italian Lamb Ragù.

Heat the oil in a shallow casserole dish over a high heat. Season the lamb with salt and pepper and fry for 6 to 8 minutes, until browned all over. Remove from the casserole dish and set aside.

Reduce the heat to medium, add the onions and fry for about 5 minutes, until softened. Add the garlic and fry for another 30 seconds.

Return the lamb to the casserole dish, add the wine and allow it to bubble for a couple of minutes. Then add the Pesto, stock and thyme. Bring everything to a simmer, cover and cook over a low heat for 1 to 1½ hours. Remove the lid and cook for a further 30 to 45 minutes, until thickened and reduced.

Towards the end of the cooking time, cook the pasta in a large pan of salted boiling water, according to the packet instructions. Drain well.

Remove the meat from the casserole and set aside. Add the cooked pasta and stir through to coat in the sauce. Divide between serving bowls and shred the meat on top of the pasta before serving.

SOFT POLENTA, PESTO MUSHROOMS AND PARMESAN

SERVES 2

1 tbsp olive oil
225 g chestnut or field
   mushrooms, sliced
150 ml hot vegetable or
   chicken stock
2 heaped tbsp Sacla' Classic
   Basil Pesto
125 g quick-cook polenta
a small knob of butter
50 g fresh Parmesan, grated
salt and freshly ground
   black pepper
fresh parsley, chopped,
   to garnish

This is comfort food at its finest, made for cold evenings or after a bracing walk. Use quick-cook polenta and the whole dish will be ready in a matter of minutes.

Heat the oil in a frying pan over a medium–high heat. Once it's nice and hot throw in the mushrooms and fry for about 5 minutes, stirring every now and then, until the mushrooms are soft and browned in places.

Pour in the stock and bubble for a few minutes, until reduced to just a couple of tablespoonfuls, then stir in the Pesto. Season with a little salt and a good grinding of pepper. Set aside and keep warm while you prepare the polenta.

Cook the polenta according to the packet instructions then stir in a little butter. Season with salt and pepper, and stir in most of the Parmesan. Spoon the polenta into warm bowls, make a little well in the middle and spoon in the hot Pesto mushrooms. Scatter with the remaining Parmesan and some chopped parsley.

CAULIFLOWER CHEESE

SERVES 2–3 AS A MAIN, 4 AS A SIDE

1 medium cauliflower, cut
    into florets
30 g plain flour
30 g butter
400–500 ml milk
100 g mature Cheddar, grated
2 tbsp chopped fresh parsley,
    plus extra to garnish
2 tbsp Sacla' Classic Basil
    Pesto
1 handful freshly grated
    Parmesan
salt and freshly ground
    black pepper

This comforting family favourite gets a special twist with some Sacla' Classic Basil Pesto. Serve as a simple supper, with a green leafy salad, or as an accompaniment to roast chicken or baked white fish.

Preheat the oven to 200°C/400°F/gas 6.

Bring a large saucepan of salted water to the boil and cook the cauliflower for 5 minutes, until just tender. Drain well and tip into a baking dish.

Meanwhile, tip the flour, butter and 400 ml milk into a large saucepan. Place over a medium heat and stir continuously with a balloon whisk for 5 to 10 minutes, until the butter has melted and the sauce starts to bubble. At this point, lower the heat right down and simmer for 5 minutes, stirring occasionally. Season with salt and pepper, then remove from the heat and stir in most of the Cheddar, reserving some for the topping. Stir in the parsley and Pesto. You want the sauce to be the consistency of double cream, so add a little more milk if needed.

Pour the sauce over the cauliflower, and sprinkle with the remaining Cheddar and the Parmesan. Place on a baking tray (to catch any drips as it cooks), and bake in the oven for 20 minutes, until golden and bubbling. Sprinkle with a little extra chopped parsley just before serving if liked.

MACARONI CHEESE WITH TENDER LEEKS AND PESTO

SERVES 2, GENEROUSLY

Slow cooked leeks add extra flavour and a touch of sophistication to this comforting childhood favourite. For a meaty version, try adding fried cubes of pancetta or bacon. A handful of chopped parsley will introduce a little more colour. This dish also works well made with wholewheat pasta – Conchiglie or Fusilli are great choices as the sauce sticks to their shapes.

200 g Macaroni
100 g Sacla' Classic Basil Pesto
1 tbsp olive oil
2 large leeks (about 300 g), sliced
25 g fresh Parmesan, grated
1 handful fresh breadcrumbs
   (optional)

for the cheese sauce

30 g plain flour
30 g butter
500–600 ml milk
100 g mature Cheddar, grated
salt and freshly ground
   black pepper

Preheat the oven to 200°C/400°F/gas 6.

In a large pan of salted boiling water, cook the pasta according to the packet instructions. Drain well, return to the hot pan and toss with the Pesto.

Meanwhile, heat the oil in a large frying pan over a medium heat and cook the leeks for 10 minutes, until softened and sweet. Mix into the macaroni.

Meanwhile, tip the flour, butter and 500 ml milk into a large saucepan. Place over a medium heat and stir continuously with a balloon whisk for 5 to 10 minutes, until the butter has melted and the sauce starts to bubble. At this point, lower the heat right down and simmer for 5 minutes, stirring occasionally. Season with salt and pepper, then remove from the heat and stir in most of the Cheddar, reserving some for the topping. You want the sauce to be the consistency of double cream, so add a little more milk if needed.

Mix the sauce and pasta together (along with some fried pancetta or bacon or chopped parsley, if using) then tip into an ovenproof dish. Sprinkle with the rest of the Cheddar, the Parmesan and breadcrumbs, if using. Place on a baking tray (to catch any drips as it cooks), and bake in the oven for 15 to 20 minutes, until golden and bubbling.

TAGLIATELLE WITH CREAMY PESTO LEEKS AND MUSHROOMS

SERVES 2

200 g Tagliatelle
1 tbsp olive oil
150 g chestnut mushrooms, sliced
1 large leek, finely sliced
150 g crème fraîche
100 g Sacla' Classic Basil Pesto
salt
fresh Parmesan, grated, to serve

A hearty dish to fill you up on a cold winter's evening. This is extra tasty with some chopped bacon – fry it together with the mushrooms.

In a large pan of salted boiling water, cook the pasta according to the packet instructions. Drain well, reserving a few spoonfuls of the cooking water.

Meanwhile, heat the oil in a large frying pan over a medium–high heat. Add the mushrooms and toss around in the hot pan for a couple of minutes, until they start to brown. Stir in the leek and lower the heat to medium. Cook gently for about 5 minutes, until sweet and soft.

Add the drained pasta to the mushrooms and leek, and stir together with the crème fraîche, Pesto and a couple of tablespoons of the pasta cooking water. Serve, scattered with plenty of Parmesan.

BAKED PESTO MEATBALLS

SERVES 4 (MAKES ABOUT 16 MEATBALLS)

500 g minced beef
⅓ large red onion, finely
    chopped (reserve the rest for
    the sauce)
50 g fresh breadcrumbs
25 g fresh Parmesan, grated
1 egg, lightly beaten
4 tbsp Sacla' Classic Basil
    Pesto
3 tbsp chopped fresh parsley
5 tbsp plain flour, seasoned
    with salt and freshly ground
    black pepper
1 tbsp olive oil

for the sauce

1 tbsp olive oil, if needed
⅔ large red onion, sliced
1 x 400 g can chopped tomatoes
2 tbsp Sacla' Sun-Dried
    Tomato, Roasted Pepper or
    Fiery Chilli Pesto (optional)
salt and freshly ground
    black pepper

For a luxurious variation, tear a 125 g ball of mozzarella into the sauce for the last 5 minutes of cooking and stir through a handful of basil leaves. Also try using Sacla' Fiery Chilli or Sun-Dried Tomato Pesto to make the meatballs. These are great served with pasta or rice.

In a large bowl, mix together all the meatball ingredients, apart from the seasoned flour and oil. Take golf-ball sized amounts of the mixture and roll into balls, then roll them in the seasoned flour, dusting off any excess.

Preheat the oven to 200°C/400°F/gas 6.

Heat the oil in a large frying pan over a medium–high heat and brown the meatballs for about 5 minutes, shaking the pan to turn them so that they brown evenly all over (you might need to do this in batches).

Tip the meatballs into a large ovenproof dish or roasting tray – they need to sit in a single layer with space all around them. Leave to one side while you make the sauce.

Pour away all but about 1 tablespoon of fat from the frying pan (if there isn't much fat in the pan then add 1 tablespoon oil). Over a medium heat, fry the sliced onion for 10 minutes, until softened and golden. Add the tomatoes and season with a little salt and pepper. Bring to a gentle simmer, stir in the Pesto, if using, then pour over the top of the meatballs. Bake in the oven for 20 minutes, until the meatballs are cooked through and the sauce has thickened and is bubbling.

CHICKEN CASSEROLE *WITH* PESTO DUMPLINGS

SERVES 4–6

2 tbsp olive oil

8 chicken thighs, on the bone

100 g pancetta cubes or smoked
  bacon lardons

1 large onion, roughly chopped

2 celery sticks, roughly
  chopped

2 carrots, peeled and roughly
  chopped

1½ tbsp plain flour

1 litre chicken stock

salt and freshly ground
  black pepper

for the dumplings

150 g self-raising flour, plus
  extra to dust

75 g vegetable suet

1 tbsp chopped fresh parsley,
  plus extra to garnish

2 tbsp Sacla' Classic Basil
  Pesto

salt and freshly ground
  black pepper

Preheat the oven to 200°C/400°F/gas 6.

Heat the oil in a large ovenproof casserole dish over a medium-high heat. Brown the chicken thighs in batches for a few minutes on each side, then remove and set aside. In the same pan, fry the pancetta or bacon lardons for a couple of minutes then stir in the vegetables and cook for about 5 minutes, until they start to brown.

Stir in the flour and cook for a minute. Pour over the stock, season with a little salt and pepper, then return the chicken pieces to the casserole dish along with any juices they have released. Bring to a simmer, cover with the lid and cook in the oven for 30 minutes.

Meanwhile, make the dumplings by mixing the flour, suet and a pinch of salt together in a bowl. Add the parsley, Pesto and about 5 tablespoons of cold water. Use your hands to bring together into a soft, but not sticky, dough (add a little extra flour, if needed). Divide the dough into eight and roll into evenly sized balls, sitting them on a lightly floured plate.

When the casserole has been in the oven for 30 minutes, remove the lid and arrange the dumplings on top. Replace the lid and cook for another 20 minutes. Remove the lid and cook for a further 10 to 15 minutes, until the dumplings are golden and the casserole is bubbling. Leave to rest for a few minutes before serving.

7

CANCEL THE TAKEAWAY

FETTUCCINE WITH ARTICHOKES, LEMON AND PESTO

SERVES 2

200 g Fettuccine

90 g Sacla' Artichoke Antipasto, roughly chopped, plus 2 tbsp of the oil

2 garlic cloves, finely sliced

100 g Sacla' Classic Basil Pesto

2 large handfuls rocket, roughly chopped

grated zest and juice of ½ a lemon

salt and freshly ground black pepper

fresh Parmesan, grated, to serve

Quick and simple, this is a perfect store-cupboard standby, but it's also smart enough for an impromptu dinner party – just double up the quantities for 4 people.

In a large pan of salted boiling water, cook the pasta according to the packet instructions. Drain well, reserving a few spoonfuls of the cooking water.

While the pasta is cooking, heat the artichokes and their oil in a large frying pan over a medium heat. When hot, add in the garlic and fry for about a minute, until you get a lovely garlicky aroma. Add the drained pasta to the pan, along with the Pesto, rocket, lemon zest and juice, and toss together to coat the pasta. Add a couple of spoonfuls of the cooking water to loosen up the sauce.

Serve with a generous sprinkling of Parmesan and lots of pepper.

ONE-MINUTE SALMON *WITH* WILD ROCKET PESTO DRESSING

SERVES 4 AS A STARTER, 2 AS A MAIN

4 tbsp Sacla' Wild Rocket
   Pesto
grated zest and juice of
   1 lemon
50 g rocket, half finely
   chopped
extra virgin olive oil,
   to drizzle
1 x 260 g chunky salmon fillet,
   sliced lengthways into
   4 evenly sliced 'fingers'
salt and freshly ground

Poaching the fish for exactly 1 minute will leave it a little soft in the middle. If you like your fish firm all the way through, give it another 30 seconds or so, depending on the thickness of the fish.

In a bowl, mix together the Pesto, lemon zest and juice and the 25 g finely chopped rocket. Season with pepper and a little oil. You're going to drizzle the sauce over the salmon, so add a little more oil if it needs loosening up.

Bring a large pan of salted water to a simmer, add the salmon and cook for exactly 1 minute, or longer if you like your fish completely cooked through. Using a slotted spoon, transfer the fish to serving plates – serve 1 piece per plate for a starter, or 2 per plate for a main course. Drizzle over the rocket dressing and top with a handful of rocket leaves.

WHITE FISH *WITH* PESTO CRUMBS *AND* GREEN BEANS   SERVES 2

3 tbsp Sacla' Sun-Dried
   Tomato Pesto
2 x 175 g chunky white fish
   fillets (haddock, pollock or
   sustainable cod)
30 g fresh breadcrumbs
1 small handful of fresh basil
   leaves, finely shredded
16 cherry tomatoes
1 tbsp olive oil, plus extra
   for greasing
salt and freshly ground
   black pepper

for the green beans

150 g green beans, stalks
   trimmed
extra virgin olive oil, to drizzle
squeeze of lemon juice

Preheat the oven to 220°C/425°F/gas 7. Spread a tablespoon of Pesto over each piece of fish and place them in a lightly greased roasting tray.

In a small bowl, mix together the remaining tablespoon of Pesto with the breadcrumbs and basil, and season with salt and pepper. Divide the mixture in two and press on top of each piece of fish to create a crust. Toss the tomatoes in the oil and scatter around the fish. Bake in the oven for 12 to 15 minutes, until the fish is just cooked through (the timings will vary slightly depending on the thickness of the fillets; have a peek in the middle using a sharp knife – the fish should be opaque and flaky).

While the fish is roasting, cook the green beans in boiling water for 2 to 3 minutes, drain and toss with a little oil and lemon juice. Arrange the beans on warm plates, sit the fish on top and serve with the tomatoes.

PESTO VEGGIE BURGER *WITH* QUICK SALSA ROSSA

MAKES 4 BURGERS

2 garlic cloves
1 x 400 g can chickpeas,
    drained
150 g Sacla' Char-Grilled
    Aubergine Pesto
100 g fresh breadcrumbs
1 large handful each fresh
    basil and flat-leaf parsley
    leaves
grated zest of 1 lemon, plus
    1 tbsp of juice
1 egg, lightly beaten
1 fresh mild chilli, halved
    lengthways, seeded and
    roughly chopped
50 g plain flour, seasoned with
    salt and freshly ground
    black pepper
3 tbsp oil
salt and freshly ground
    black pepper

for the salsa rossa

200 g cherry or baby plum
    tomatoes, cut into quarters
1 handful fresh basil leaves,
    roughly chopped
3 tbsp Sacla' Char-Grilled
    Peppers Antipasto, chopped,
    plus 1 tbsp of the oil

Put the garlic into a food processor and blitz until finely chopped. Tip in the chickpeas, Pesto, 75 g of the breadcrumbs, the herbs, lemon zest and juice, the egg and chilli. Season with salt and pepper, and blitz again until just combined to a rough texture.

Divide the mixture into four and, with lightly floured hands, shape into burgers. The mixture might be a bit soft, so don't worry if your burgers aren't perfectly round.

Combine the remaining 25 g of breadcrumbs and the seasoned flour on a plate then lightly drop the burgers into the mixture and coat well. You can cook the burgers straight away, but if you have time pop them in the fridge on the breadcrumb plate to firm up for about 20 minutes.

Preheat the oven to 200°C/400°F/gas 6.

Heat the oil in a large frying pan over a medium–high heat and fry the burgers for 4 minutes on each side, then finish them off on a baking tray in the oven for about 10 minutes.

Mix all the salsa rossa ingredients together and serve with the burgers.

FRESH TROFIE WITH POTATOES AND PESTO

SERVES 2

300 g Sacla' Trofie pasta
1 medium potato (about 250 g),
    peeled and cut into 1 cm-
    cubes
100 g green beans, cut into
    4 cm-pieces
100 g Sacla' Classic Basil Pesto,
    or 150 g Sacla' Fresh Classic
    Basil Pesto
fresh Parmesan, grated,
    to serve
salt and freshly ground
    black pepper

*Make sure you use a really big pan for this recipe –
you'll need plenty of room for the potato and beans to
cook with the pasta.*

Bring a large pan of well-salted water to the boil.
Cook the pasta according to the packet instructions,
adding the potato cubes 6 minutes before the end of
the cooking time. (If you're using Sacla' Trofie Fresh
Pasta, which takes 10 minutes, you'll need to add the
potatoes after 4 minutes.) Cook the potatoes with the
pasta for 3 minutes, then add the beans. Cook for
another 3 minutes, then drain, reserving a few
tablespoons of the cooking water. Return the pasta,
potatoes and beans to the hot pan.

Stir in the Pesto with a splash of the cooking water
until everything is mixed together. Season and serve,
scattered generously with grated Parmesan.

LINGUINE WITH PRAWNS AND PESTO

BY JANE CURRAN

SERVES 2

150 g Linguine
6 medium tomatoes
2 tsp olive oil
125 g cooked prawns, shelled
1 tbsp Sacla' Classic Basil Pesto
salt and freshly ground black pepper
fresh basil leaves, to garnish

This recipe from Jane Curran, the Cookery Editor of woman&home *magazine, is delicious and takes no time at all to make.*

In a large pan of salted boiling water, cook the pasta according to the packet instructions.

Meanwhile, halve the tomatoes and scoop out and discard the seeds with a spoon. Finely dice the tomatoes. About 4 minutes before the pasta is ready, heat the oil in a frying pan over a medium heat and add the tomatoes. Season with salt and pepper and toss together to heat through. Be careful not to let them become mushy. Now, simply stir in the prawns and Pesto, heat through for 3 to 4 minutes and then add the drained pasta. Sprinkle with the basil and serve immediately.

RIGATONI *WITH* SPEEDY GRATED COURGETTE SAUCE

SERVES 4

400 g Rigatoni
4 tbsp olive oil
4 courgettes, coarsely grated
3 garlic cloves, finely chopped
1½ tbsp dried chilli flakes
190 g Sacla' Classic Basil Pesto
salt and freshly ground
   black pepper
fresh Parmesan, grated,
   to serve

The sauce cooks in the time it takes to boil the pasta, making this a perfect quick supper.

In a large pan of salted boiling water, cook the pasta according to the packet instructions.

While the pasta is cooking, heat the oil in a large frying pan over a medium–high heat and fry the courgettes for 8 to 10 minutes, until they start to turn golden-brown. Throw in the garlic and chilli and toss everything together for a couple of minutes, until you start to get a lovely garlicky aroma. Turn the heat down to low and stir in the Pesto.

When the pasta is ready, drain it, reserving a little of the cooking water. Toss the hot pasta into the courgette mixture, along with a couple of spoonfuls of the pasta cooking water. Season with salt and pepper, and serve with plenty of grated Parmesan.

QUICK PESTO PIZZA MAKES 12 MINI PIZZAS

6 mini pitta breads, split
    in half and lightly toasted
Sacla' Classic Basil, Sun-Dried
    Tomato or Fiery Chilli Pesto
125 g ball of mozzarella, torn
    into pieces

your choice from the
    following:

cherry tomatoes, cut into
    quarters
red and yellow peppers, finely
    diced
anchovies
stoned olives, halved
Italian ham, torn into pieces
slices of salami

Mix and match different Pesto varieties and toppings so there's something for everyone. Try Classic Basil Pesto with cherry tomatoes, Sun-Dried Tomato Pesto with diced peppers and ham or anchovies, and Fiery Chilli Pesto with salami. Don't overload the ingredients or else they won't cook properly, and stick to just two or three toppings.

Preheat the oven 220°C/425°F/gas 7.

Spread each pitta half with a heaped teaspoon of Pesto. Sprinkle with your choice of toppings and scatter with mozzarella. Cook in the oven for 5 to 7 minutes, until the cheese has melted and is starting to bubble.

PESTO BAKED POTATOES *with* MELTING MOZZARELLA SERVES 4

4 baking potatoes
olive oil, to drizzle
25 g salted butter
4 tbsp Sacla' Classic Basil
    Pesto
2 tbsp freshly grated
    Parmesan, plus extra
    for sprinkling
2 tbsp double cream
1 tbsp finely chopped
    fresh chives
125 g ball of mozzarella
salt and freshly ground
    black pepper

This weeknight staple is flexible and can be adapted to make use of ingredients you already have. Try adding fried chopped onions; mushrooms; bacon or cubes of pancetta; herbs, such as parsley or basil; and other cheeses that melt well, like fontina or provolone.

Preheat the oven to 200°C/400°F/gas 6. Prick the potatoes with a fork, rub with a little oil and salt, and bake directly on the oven shelf for about 1 hour, depending on their size. Squeeze, and if they feel soft, they're ready!

Using oven gloves, remove the potatoes from the oven, cut them in half and scoop out the middles into a bowl. Mash the potato with the butter, Pesto, Parmesan, cream and chives, and season with salt and pepper. Mix in any other ingredients you're using (see introduction) and return the mixture to the potato shells: Place the filled potatoes in a baking dish, tear over the mozzarella and sprinkle with Parmesan. Drizzle with a little oil and return to the oven for about 10 minutes, until bubbling and golden.

SICILIAN-STYLE PENNE *WITH* AUBERGINES *AND* ORGANIC PESTO

SERVES 2

200 g Penne
4 tbsp olive oil
1 medium onion, finely sliced
1 small aubergine, cut into
    2 cm-dice
pinch of dried chilli flakes
100 g Sacla' Organic Tomato
    Pesto
1 tbsp chopped fresh flat-leaf
    parsley
salt
fresh Parmesan, grated,
    to serve

Take the time to caramelise the onions slowly and get the aubergines nice and soft, and you'll be rewarded with a simple dish that's packed full of flavour.

In a large pan of salted boiling water, cook the pasta according to the packet instructions. Drain, reserving about 4 tablespoons of the cooking water.

Heat 1 tablespoon of the oil in a large frying pan over a medium heat and fry the onion for about 5 minutes, until soft and golden. Transfer the onion to a plate then add the remaining 3 tablespoons of oil to the pan and increase the heat to high. Add the aubergine and toss in the hot oil. Cook for 5 minutes, stirring occasionally, until browned on all sides, then pour in a splash (about 50 ml) of boiling water and let it bubble and steam the aubergine. Once the water has boiled off, sprinkle some salt over the aubergine and cook for a further 2 to 4 minutes until it's nice and soft. Return the onion to the pan, along with the chilli flakes, Pesto, parsley and the pasta, and gently stir together. Add a little of the cooking water to loosen the sauce, then serve with plenty of grated Parmesan.

FRESH ORECCHIETTE *WITH* BROCCOLI *AND* FIERY CHILLI PESTO

SERVES 2–3

300 g Sacla' Orecchiette pasta
150 g tenderstem broccoli or purple sprouting broccoli, chopped into 4 cm-lengths, or 150 g broccoli, cut into florets
2 tbsp olive oil
3 garlic cloves, finely sliced
100 g Sacla' Fiery Chilli Pesto
salt
fresh Parmesan, grated, to serve

A quick and colourful pasta dish – from cupboard to table in 10 minutes.

In a large pan of salted boiling water, cook the pasta according to the packet instructions. About 3 minutes before the end of the cooking time, throw in the broccoli. Drain the pasta and broccoli, reserving a few tablespoons of the cooking water. Return to the hot pan.

Heat the oil in a large frying pan over a medium heat, add the garlic and cook for a couple of minutes until golden and fragrant, taking care not to let it burn.

Add the pasta and broccoli to the garlic and toss together for a minute, then stir in the Pesto and a few tablespoons of the cooking water to loosen the sauce. (If your frying pan is too small to hold all the pasta, toss half of it at a time in the garlic oil and return it to the pasta pan before adding the Pesto.) Serve with lots of freshly grated Parmesan.

8

HOME COMFORTS

PESTO SALMON FISH FINGERS

MAKES 6–8 FISH FINGERS

2 tsp olive oil, plus extra
    for greasing
25 g plain flour
1 egg
50 g fresh breadcrumbs
2 tbsp Sacla' Classic Basil
    Pesto
1 tbsp freshly grated Parmesan
1 tbsp chopped fresh parsley
1 x 200 g salmon fillet, cut into
    6–8 chunky 'fingers'
salt and freshly ground
    black pepper

Kids and grown-ups will love these crispy fish fingers! Serve them with peas and mashed potatoes or between thick slices of white bread for a fish finger sandwich with a twist. These are also great served as a nibble with drinks. If you prefer, you can use a meaty white fish, such as haddock or pollock.

Preheat the oven to 200°C/400°F/gas 6. Lightly grease a baking tray with a little oil.

Put the flour in a shallow bowl and season with salt and pepper. Lightly whisk the egg in a second shallow bowl. Mix the breadcrumbs, Pesto, Parmesan, parsley and oil together in a third shallow bowl. Line up the bowls in front of you.

Take a salmon finger and coat it first in the seasoned flour, then dip it in the egg. Finally, roll it in the Pesto breadcrumbs, pressing them on firmly. Place the coated salmon on the greased baking tray and repeat with the rest of the fish. Pop them in the oven for 10 minutes, turn them over and give them another 5 to 10 minutes, until nice and golden-brown and crisp. Transfer to kitchen paper to absorb any excess oil, and serve.

BAKED PASTA TRICOLORE

SERVES 4

400 g Sacla' Conchiglie pasta

190 g Sacla' Roasted Pepper Pesto

175 g Sacla' Char-Grilled Peppers Antipasto, plus 3 tbsp of the oil

2 tbsp olive oil

1 large onion, chopped

3 garlic cloves, finely chopped

2 x 400 g cans chopped tomatoes

200 g fresh baby spinach leaves

125 g ball of mozzarella, roughly torn

30 g fresh Parmesan, grated

salt and freshly ground black pepper

If you love mozzarella then use an extra 125 g ball, roughly torn, and stir it through when you add the pasta to the sauce.

Preheat the oven to 200°C/400°F/gas 6.

In a large pan of salted boiling water, cook the pasta according to the packet instructions. Drain well, reserving a few spoonfuls of the cooking water then return to the hot pan and stir in the Pesto and peppers.

Heat the olive oil in a large frying pan over a medium–high heat. Add the onion and fry for 10 minutes, until softened and golden then chuck in the garlic and cook for a minute – be careful not to let the garlic burn. Add the tomatoes, bring to a simmer and cook for 15 minutes.

Season well with salt and pepper, then gently stir in the spinach. Cover with a lid and cook for a minute or two until the spinach has wilted.

Stir in the pasta mixture, check and adjust the seasoning, then tip everything into a baking dish. Scatter with the torn mozzarella and Parmesan and drizzle with the oil from the peppers. Bake in the oven for 10 to 15 minutes until golden and bubbling.

SPAGHETTI MARINARA

SERVES 4

400 g Spaghetti
2 tbsp olive oil
3 garlic cloves, finely chopped
a good pinch of dried chilli
  flakes
400 g seafood mix (mussels,
  squid and prawns)
125 ml white wine
1 large handful fresh flat-leaf
  parsley leaves
190 g Sacla' Organic Tomato
  Pesto
salt and freshly ground
  black pepper

In a large pan of salted boiling water, cook the pasta according to the packet instructions. Drain well, reserving a few spoonfuls of the cooking water then return the pasta to the hot pan.

Heat the oil in a large frying pan over a medium heat, add the garlic and chilli and fry for 2 minutes until golden, taking care not to let the garlic burn. Increase the heat to high and stir in the seafood. Keep stirring for 2 minutes then pour over the wine and let it bubble for a couple more minutes. Lower the heat right down and simmer for 2 to 3 minutes, until the sauce is steaming hot and the seafood is cooked through.

Add the seafood and its liquid to the pasta along with the parsley and mix well, then stir in the Pesto. Season with salt and pepper and serve immediately.

VEGETABLE BAKE WITH PESTO 'CRUMBLE' TOPPING

SERVES 4

1 large aubergine, cut into
    2 cm-chunks
1 large red onion, cut into
    wedges
3 courgettes, halved
    lengthways and cut into
    2 cm-half moons
3 red peppers, cut into
    3 cm-chunks
1 x 250 g sweet potato, peeled
    and thinly sliced
5 garlic cloves, roughly chopped
5 tbsp olive oil
2 x 400 g cans chopped
    tomatoes
100 g Sacla' Sun-Dried Tomato
    Pesto
salt and freshly ground
    black pepper

for the topping

30 g wholemeal flour
30 g butter
30 g fresh Ciabatta (or other
    fresh) breadcrumbs
30 g mixed seeds
15 g pine nuts, toasted
45 g fresh Parmesan, grated
2 tbsp Sacla' Classic Basil
    Pesto
salt and freshly ground
    black pepper

Preheat the oven to 200°C/400°F/gas 6.

Tip all the vegetables into a large, deep roasting tray, toss together with the garlic and oil, and season with salt and pepper. Roast for 45 minutes, stirring once, until they start to brown, then pour over the tomatoes and Pesto. Return to the oven for 15 minutes.

Meanwhile, make the crumble topping by pulsing the flour and butter in a food processor until it comes together into rough crumbs, then chuck in everything else, apart from the Pesto. Pulse to just combine. Add the Pesto and pulse just once or twice to mix together, be careful not to over mix, as you want it crumbly, not sticking together like a dough. (If you don't have a food processor, you can rub the butter into the flour by hand. Roughly chop the seeds and pine nuts and add them along with all the other ingredients.)

Scatter the crumble topping over the vegetables and bake for another 15 to 20 minutes until golden and crunchy.

PESTO MASH SERVES 4

1 kg potatoes, peeled and cut
    into rough chunks
75 ml milk
40 g butter
100 g Sacla' Classic Basil Pesto
extra virgin olive oil, for
    drizzling
salt

For a little extra indulgence, add a large handful of freshly grated Parmesan cheese or some fried cubes of pancetta or smoked bacon. This is absolutely delicious served alongside roast chicken or sausages.

Boil the potatoes in a large pan of salted water for 10 to 12 minutes, until tender. Drain well then return the potatoes to the hot pan and heat over a low heat for a few seconds to dry off any excess water.

Add the milk, butter and Pesto and mash together over a low heat until smooth. Serve, drizzled with a little olive oil. So easy!

PORK CHOPS WITH A PESTO CRUST SERVES 2

2 x 250 g thick pork chops
olive oil, to drizzle
salt and freshly ground
    black pepper

for the Pesto crust
30 g walnuts, finely chopped
40 g fresh breadcrumbs
4 tbsp chopped fresh flat-
    leaf parsley
8 stoned green olives,
    finely chopped
grated zest of 1 lemon
3 tbsp Sacla' Classic Basil
    Pesto

Serve with creamy mashed potatoes and some green vegetables or a salad.

Preheat the oven to 200°C/400°F/gas 6.

Rub the pork chops all over with a little oil and season with salt and pepper. Heat a frying pan over a medium-high heat and fry the pork chops for 2 minutes on each side until nicely brown.

Mix all the Pesto crust ingredients together in a shallow dish. Make 2 piles of the crumbs in a roasting tray, each using about a tablespoon of the mixture. Sit a pork chop on top of each. Cover with the remaining Pesto crust so it's piled high, drizzle with oil and roast in the oven for 10 to 12 minutes, until the pork is cooked through.

ROASTED TOMATO AND BACON PASTA

BY KAREN BARNES

SERVES 4

600 g cherry tomatoes, halved
olive oil, to drizzle
400 g Penne
200 g bacon lardons (or you can use snipped-up streaky bacon, or even pieces of chorizo)
75 g pine nuts
1 tbsp Sacla' Classic Basil Pesto (or more, to taste)
1 large handful fresh basil leaves, torn, plus extra to garnish
salt and freshly ground black pepper
fresh Parmesan, grated, to serve

Karen Barnes is a passionate cook as well as Editor of delicious *magazine. Karen says, 'I always have a couple of boxes of cherry tomatoes in the fridge to make this incredibly quick stand-by supper. If your tomatoes taste a bit bland and watery, you can liven up the flavour with a light sprinkling of caster sugar before putting them in the oven'.*

Preheat the oven to 200°C/400°F/gas 6. Bring a large pan of salted water to the boil.

Arrange the tomato halves in a large roasting tray, cut-side up. Drizzle with oil and season with plenty of pepper. Cook in the oven for about 15 minutes, until they're starting to collapse and caramelise. Meanwhile, cook the pasta in the boiling water according to the packet instructions.

While the tomatoes and pasta are cooking, heat a frying pan over a medium–high heat and tip in the lardons (you don't need to add any oil). Fry for a few minutes, until they start to crisp up. Add the pine nuts and toss with the lardons until they turn golden. Remove from the heat.

When the pasta is ready, drain thoroughly and return to the hot pan. Stir in the tomatoes and all their juices, then add the lardons and pine nuts, and a little of the oil from the frying pan (don't add too much). Stir in a generous dollop of Pesto and the basil leaves. Mix well and season, to taste, with salt and pepper. Serve right away with plenty of Parmesan and a few more basil leaves.

INDEX

THE SACLA' RANGE

We are the original Pesto Pioneers but we
also make a whole range of authentic
Italian foods in our kitchens in Italy.

Full details of our complete range is
available on our website www.sacla.co.uk
but meanwhile here is a selection of our
most popular recipes to whet your appetite.

PESTO

The original Pesto is made with fresh basil leaves, olive oil, Grana Padano and pine nuts and it's become so popular that we have created ten delicious recipes to keep in your cupboard. What's more, you'll find four more recipes in a chilled pouch, for dinner tonight, and two flavours in a squeezy bottle.

Choose from this delicious selection:

Char-Grilled Aubergine
  (recipe pages: 18–19, 92–3 & 124–5)
Classic Basil*
  (recipe pages: 10–13, 18–19, 24–5, 30–9, 42–7, 50–9, 62–77, 80–91, 98–103, 106–121, 126–33, 140–1 & 146–51)
Fiery Chilli*
  (recipe pages: 12–15, 22–3, 26–7, 34–5, 56–7, 114–15, 132–3 & 136–7)
Fresh Coriander
  (recipe pages: 16–17, 28–9 & 96–7)
Fresh Spicy Roasted Pepper*
  (recipe pages: 104–5)
Fresh Tomato & Olive*
Organic Basil
Organic Tomato
  (recipe pages: 22–3, 26–7, 134–5 & 144–5)
Roasted Pepper
  (recipe pages: 12–13, 114–15 & 142–3)
Sun-Dried Tomato*
  (recipe pages: 12–13, 34–5, 40–1, 60–3, 78–9, 98–9, 114–15, 122–3, 132–3 & 146–7)
Wild Garlic
Wild Rocket
  (recipe pages: 48–9 & 122–3)

PASTA

Our sauces have a lifelong partner in our range of Sacla' Pasta, created to hold every drop of your favourite Sacla' sauce.

Our dried Pasta is made in Puglia in Southern Italy from Italian durum wheat and was selected by the Sacla' family for its superior flavour, texture and character. We shape the pasta dough through a traditional bronze die to give it a textured surface, which will hold every drop of the pasta sauce you choose to use. Then we dry it very slowly to protect and preserve all the flavour and goodness of this favourite Italian food. Put simply, this is pasta as it should be.

Conchiglie
  (recipe pages: 84–5 & 102–3)
Fusilli
Penne Giganti

Our fresh Pasta, which you will find in the chilled cabinet, comes in two traditional shapes.

Orecchiette
  (recipe pages 92–3 & 136–7)
Trofie
  (recipe pages 52–3, 104–5 & 126–7)

*also available in the chiller cabinet

ANTIPASTI

Italians serve antipasti before the meal, quite simply, with meat and cheese. These are the perfect store cupboard standby to help you bring Italian magic to your favourite dishes.

Artichoke
   (recipe pages: 44–5, 120–1)
Char-Grilled Peppers
   (recipe pages: 10–11, 14–15, 26–7, 64–5, 124–5 & 142–3)
Mixed Beans with Mushrooms
Peperonata
Sun-Dried Tomato
   (recipe pages 40–1, 44–5 & 62–3)
Wild Mushroom

WHOLE CHERRY TOMATO

Our Whole Cherry Tomato Pasta Sauces start with an authentic soffritto base of celery, carrots, garlic and onion to which we add whole (yes, whole!) cherry tomatoes and one other special ingredient to give each sauce its amazing character.

Whole Cherry Tomato & Basil
Whole Cherry Tomato & Chilli
Whole Cherry Tomato & Parmesan
Whole Cherry Tomato & Roasted
   Vegetables

INTENSE SAUCES

Packed with flavour and made with the finest Italian ingredients, these sauces are the closest you can get to homemade and they are what the Italians eat in Italy. Made in Italy, by Italians, for Italians you could say!

Choose from this delicious selection:

Tomato & Olive*
Tomato & Mascarpone
Tomato & Garlic
Tomato & Chilli
Spicy Tomato & Pepper*
Tomato & Rocket
Red Onion & Gorgonzola

*also available in the chiller cabinet

ACKNOWLEDGEMENTS

This book is for the team of Pesto Pioneers in Italy and the UK who are so enduringly passionate about this little piece of Italian magic.

Over the years we've been helped, supported and hugely inspired by chefs and food writers and their boundless passion for creating delicious Italian food. Our thanks to them all and to those who have shared their recipes with us here:
Dhruv Baker, Karen Barnes, Anna del Conte, Jane Curran, Henrietta Green, Lucas Hollweg, Helena Lang, Theo Randall, Phil Vickery, Lorna Wing, and Antony Worrall Thompson.